Food For Thought

By Susan Schott Karr

CELEBRATION PRESS
Pearson Learning Group

Contents

Beginning With Pasta

Every living thing, including people, must eat some kind of food in order to survive. Throughout history, people have invented a variety of ways to prepare food to make eating more interesting. In this book, you'll learn about some of the most popular tasty treats—pasta, cheese, popcorn, potatoes, peanut butter, and chocolate. You will also learn a little about the history of these foods.

Spaghetti is a fun food to eat.

When you eat a dish of pasta, you might name it by the shape of the noodles. Penne, ziti, spaghetti, tubettini—pasta comes in all shapes and sizes. It might be red or green or white. It might look like a curly spring or a bow tie. You might like to eat it with tomato sauce or cheese sauce. You might like it with just a bit of butter and a sprinkling of grated Parmesan cheese.

Pasta is made by mixing flour, water, eggs, and salt into a paste. The word *pasta* even means "paste"! Then the dough is cut into shapes and dried.

During Medieval times (about 800 to 1500), people used the word *macaroni* to describe what we now call pasta. Today, most people think of macaroni as a curly tube, such as elbow noodles. Back then, macaroni meant any shape or size of noodle.

People do not always agree about the origins of pasta. The Italian and the Chinese people each claim to have made the first pasta. One story says that Marco Polo found pasta in China and brought it back to Italy. Another story says that what Marco Polo discovered was that the Chinese had a pasta similar to that of his native Italy.

Long ago, pasta was hung on long poles to dry in the sun.

Thomas Jefferson may have introduced the pasta machine to America. In 1787, Jefferson came home from Italy with a macaroni machine. He had his staff add cheddar cheese to pasta and then bake it to make macaroni and cheese.

In 1848, a Frenchman named Antoine Zerega opened the first American pasta factory in New York. His machines were operated with the pulling power of one horse. The freshly made pasta was laid on the roof to dry in the sun.

Say Cheese

Swiss cheese, blue cheese, string cheese, Jack cheese—there are so many kinds of cheese to choose from. Cheese can be hard, soft, round, square, white, orange, yellow, or even stinky. It can have lines of blue mold in it. Cheese can melt in your mouth in a gooey grilled cheese sandwich. It can stretch like a rubber band from your plate to your chin when it's on a hot pizza.

Cheese is made at the Haastrecht Farm near Gouda in The Netherlands.

Making cheese is a craft people have been practicing for thousands of years. For example, **ancient** Egyptian murals painted on tomb walls dating from 3100 B.C. show people making cheese. Some **archaeologists** also believe they have found the remains of cheese in tomb jars.

One legend of how cheese was discovered tells of an Arab merchant. He set out on a trip across the desert 4,000 years ago. He carried milk in a bag made from a sheep's stomach. When he arrived at his destination, the merchant discovered that the milk had curdled or separated into a kind of cheese. An **enzyme** called rennet in the lining of the sheep's stomach combined with the sun's heat. The combination caused the liquid to turn into curds and whey! The curds are the cheese, similar to cottage cheese. The whey is the leftover liquid.

Cheese making came to America in 1492 with the explorer Christopher Columbus, who brought the first cows to the Americas on his ship. When the *Mayflower* set sail from England in 1620, there was plenty of aged, or hard, cheese on board. There were also dairy goats to make more. It was in these ways that cheese came to America.

Easy Pizza

Frozen bread or pizza dough can be found in most grocery stores or in bakeries. Be sure to ask an adult to help you. You will need:

1 package frozen bread or pizza dough	1 cup grated mozzarella cheese
olive oil	toppings
1 cup tomato sauce	pizza pan or cookie sheet

Directions

1. Defrost the dough according to the directions on the package.
2. Spread some olive oil over the dough.
3. Heat the oven to 450°F.
4. Place the dough on a cookie sheet or pizza pan, then flatten and stretch it to fit the pan.
5. Spread the tomato sauce on the dough.
6. Sprinkle the cheese on top.
7. Top with any toppings that you like.
8. Bake for about 10 minutes, or according to the directions on the package.
9. Enjoy!

Pizza is one food that contains a lot of cheese. In 1830, the first pizza restaurant opened in Naples, Italy. The modern tomato-and-cheese pizza appeared in Naples in 1889. A chef named Don Raffaele Esposito prepared a pizza for the visiting king and queen of Italy, using tomatoes, basil, and mozzarella to represent the colors of the Italian flag.

Behind the "Pop" in Popcorn

Americans eat about 17.3 billion quarts of popcorn each year. Popcorn lovers have their favorite kind of popcorn. Many people love crazy flavors such as chocolate, butter toffee, or chili.

There are many different kinds of corn. Sweet corn is the type of corn that people usually eat as corn-on-the-cob or cooked corn. Feed corn is for animals. Rice corn and pearl corn are for popping.

Popcorn is a popular snack at sports events.

Corn with good "poppability" has a high amount of starch. The kernels have a hard coat or outside, and a soft, moist inside. Farmers wait to harvest popcorn until the kernels are hard. Next, the kernels are dried, then shelled from the cobs.

Popping happens when the kernels are heated. As the moisture inside the kernel turns to steam, the pulpy heart swells. Finally, the outer shell bursts, or pops open, showing the fluffy, white inside.

The first corn was **cultivated** about 7,000 years ago in Mexico. The oldest known cobs of American popping corn were found in 1948 and 1950 in a bat cave in New Mexico. Scientists think that the cobs were about 5,600 years old. Some of the ears were smaller than a penny. Others were as long as 2 inches.

Scientists also have dug up ears of popcorn more than 1,000 years old that still looked fresh and white. They tried heating some of the kernels and discovered that they still popped.

By the first century B.C., corn was the main **staple** food in the Americas. In 1492, Columbus found native Americans selling jewelry made of dried popcorn kernels.

A Navajo woman carries freshly picked corn.

Native Americans prepared popcorn in many ways. Some groups speared the dried corn cobs with sticks and held them over the fire until the kernels popped on the cob. The Iroquois people put corn in clay pots filled with hot sand. They stirred the sand until the kernels popped.

Popcorn may have been the first breakfast cereal. In America, English **colonists** and later pioneers ate popcorn with cream poured over it for breakfast. Sometimes they added sugar.

In 1885, Charles Cretors of Chicago, Illinois, invented a gas-powered popcorn popper. Soon, vendors pushing their popcorn machines in parks and at fairs were a common sight. In the early part of the twentieth century, the popcorn machines moved inside when movie theaters were opened.

In the 1950s, popcorn sales rose along with the number of television sets. Popcorn was no longer just for movie theaters. People happily stayed home, watched television, and ate popcorn. This is still true today.

Hot Potatoes

The potato is an important vegetable. It is loaded with vitamins and minerals, making it a good source of **nutrition**. When eaten without anything added, it is a low-calorie, fat-free food. However, Americans tend to love potatoes in their high-fat forms—potato chips and french fries. For example, the typical person in the United States eats about 16 pounds of french fries each year.

Two women check the quality of chips in a potato chip factory.

The potato was first cultivated in Peru about 1,800 years ago. The Incas lived high in the Andes Mountains—too high to grow maize, another name for corn. They grew potatoes instead. Their potatoes came in many colors and shapes. Some were red or gold and others were blue or black. Some were small and round like grapes. Others were long and thin, like fingers. Some even looked like the potatoes we usually see in the store today.

In 1537, Spanish soldiers discovered potatoes growing in an Andean village. When they found out how tasty potatoes were, they took potatoes back to Spain. At first, Europeans were suspicious of the new vegetable because it is related to nightshade plants, which are poisonous. However, the potato was slowly accepted, and in time it became a staple food in Spain and Ireland.

Benjamin Franklin made the potato popular in America. He returned from France telling of a dinner he had attended at which the potato was served 20 different ways. It wasn't long before potatoes were being grown in the colonies and in the western frontier.

A woman and child harvest potatoes near Cuzco, Peru.

French fries remain the most popular form of potatoes in the United States. *French* means "to cut in long strips." President Thomas Jefferson introduced french fries to America when he served them at the White House.

Today, the American french fry has returned to its potato roots. You can now buy blue french fries in the grocery store. They are made from blue potatoes, **descendants** of the same kind of potatoes the ancient Incans grew.

Peanut Butter Lovers

Have you eaten 5 pounds of peanut butter yet this year? That's how much peanut butter an average American eats. In total, Americans eat 700 million pounds of peanut butter each year.

Peanuts are not nuts. Nuts grow on trees, but peanuts don't. Peanuts are a type of vegetable called legumes, which are seeds you can eat that grow in **pods**. Other legumes are peas, beans, and lentils.

George Washington Carver found more than 300 ways to use the peanut plant.

Peanuts grow underground, but they are very different from root plants such as potatoes. After the peanut flowers bloom, they lose their petals. The stem grows down toward the ground. The budding peanut pod at the tip of the stem works its way into the ground. There, the pod ripens and forms a shell around the peanuts inside.

Peanuts grow best in warm climates. Archaeologists believe peanuts started in present-day Bolivia, South America, where wild peanuts still grow. Today, the largest peanut producers are China, India, and the United States.

Native Americans in South America were the first to make peanut butter. They ground peanuts into a sticky paste. Then they mixed it with cocoa (kō kō), the main ingredient in chocolate. This South American treat may have been the world's first chocolate-peanut candy.

In the 1500s, Portuguese explorers carried peanuts from South America to Asia, Europe, and Africa. Enslaved Africans were the first to cultivate peanuts in North America. From the African Kimbundu word for peanut, *nguba*, comes the word *goober*, a southern nickname for peanuts.

It wasn't until 1890 that modern peanut butter appeared in the United States. An unknown doctor in St. Louis, Missouri, was looking for something high in protein and inexpensive. He wanted to give people with bad teeth, who had a hard time chewing meat, a high-protein substitute.

The doctor began to grind peanuts into a paste that could be spread on bread. At first, he used a meat grinder that he cranked by hand in his home. Then he started a food-products company owned by George A. Bayle Jr. to grind peanuts and package his peanut butter. This modern food was sold for about 6 cents per pound.

Even with peanut butter, the demand for peanuts remained low. Then around 1900 equipment was invented to plant and harvest peanuts. The greatest boost to the peanut industry came from Dr. George Washington Carver. In 1903, Carver began to study peanuts in Alabama. He came up with more than 300 ways to use the peanut plant, including making paper, ink, and oils. Today, Carver is known as the father of the peanut industry.

Georgia is now the state that grows the most peanuts in the United States. Farmers harvest about 26 million tons of peanuts a year. An acre of peanut plants produces enough peanuts to make 30,000 peanut butter sandwiches!

More Peanut and Peanut Butter Facts

- March is National Peanut Month.

- Two U.S. presidents were peanut farmers—Thomas Jefferson and Jimmy Carter.

- About 550 peanuts are needed to make a 12-ounce jar of creamy peanut butter.

- People in the western United States like chunky peanut butter. People in the eastern United States like creamy peanut butter.

- Researchers are working to remove the proteins from peanuts that cause allergic reactions.

Chocolate by Choice

Chocolate bars, chocolate cake, chocolate milk, chocolate pudding—there are so many ways to enjoy chocolate. Entire cookbooks have been written about chocolate. It is one of the oldest treats. The Olmecs in Mexico may have had chocolate nearly 2,400 years ago. Chocolate was also discovered in a Mayan tomb in Honduras. Scientists believe it is more than 1,500 years old.

Soldiers enjoy chocolate during World War I.

Cocoa is the main ingredient in chocolate. Cocoa by itself is bitter. Chocolate tastes sweet because of added ingredients such as sugar and cream. As far back as the 1300s, the Aztec people in Mexico drank cocoa as a bitter beverage.

The Aztecs made their drink by roasting the cocoa beans and adding water but not sugar. Sometimes they added vanilla or even spicy chili peppers. Only rich people could afford this special drink, which they called *chocolatl*.

The Aztecs also used cocoa beans as a form of money to **barter** for other goods. A tomato was worth one cocoa bean. An avocado was worth two cocoa beans. A "good turkey hen" was worth 100 cocoa beans.

In the early 1500s, the Spanish people discovered the "magic beans" that the Aztecs were growing. One Spanish explorer brought some of the beans back to the king and queen of Spain. In Spain, people did not like the dark, bitter drink that the Aztecs drank. They added sugar and sometimes cinnamon to make a delicious drink of their own. Sometimes they added black pepper instead of spicy chilies.

The Cocoa Plant

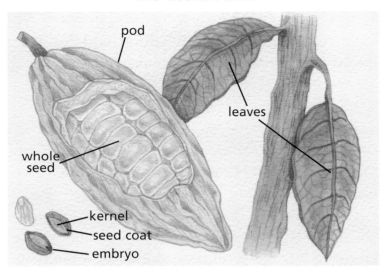

The Spanish people kept their secret of how to process and prepare chocolate for nearly 100 years. Pirates who captured Spanish ships filled with cocoa beans didn't know what a valuable cargo they had seized. They thought the beans were sheep droppings and threw them overboard!

Chocolate became popular in Europe in the 1600s. People began meeting in chocolate houses to discuss politics and drink a cup of chocolate, coffee, or tea.

A new type of steam engine patented by James Watt in 1769 added greatly to the chocolate industry. Soon, it was possible to grind large quantities of cocoa beans to make chocolate powder. In 1847, an English company found a way to create chocolate paste that could be molded and hardened. People began to think about eating chocolate as well as drinking it.

In 1893, an American from Pennsylvania named Milton Hershey entered the chocolate business. In 1900, he introduced his Hershey milk chocolate bar. Five years later came the chocolate kiss. By 1907, his business had grown so big that he took over the town of Derry Church and renamed it Hershey.

During World War II, it was Hershey's idea to add chocolate to soldiers' **rations**. Hershey made bars that were less likely to melt. Chocolate became a quick source of energy, and a little taste of home for the soldiers.

Chocolate, popcorn, pasta, potatoes, peanut butter, and cheese are just a few of the foods people love to eat. In the future, there may be new ways to eat these foods or even new foods.

Glossary

ancient belonging to the distant past before A.D. 476.

archaeologists scientists who study ancient times and peoples by examining what is left of their buildings, tools, and other things

barter to trade one thing for another without using money

colonists early European settlers of North America

cultivated grown as crops

descendants those who come after a certain ancestor

enzyme a complex protein made by living cells

nutrition the process of nourishing or being nourished

pods protective containers

rations food given out to members of a group

staple a main product that is grown, produced, or eaten in a region